Bernadette Baldelli

BLACKWORK EMBROIDERY

STITCHES, TECHNIQUES AND 13 MODERN PROJECTS

Thank you to Milpoint for the fabric and
Maison Sajou for the yarn.

First published in Great Britain in 2020 by
Search Press Limited
Wellwood, North Farm Road,
Tunbridge Wells, Kent TN2 3DR

© LIBELLA, Paris, 2018

This translation of BLACKWORK, first published in France by LIBELLA under the imprint LTA in 2018, is published by arrangement with Silke Bruenink Agency, Munich, Germany.

English Translation by Burravoe Translation Services

Photographs: Fabrice Besse
Styling: Sonia Roy
Photogravure: Nord Compo

ISBN 978-1-78221-811-1

18
Moth-patterned pillows

34
Camellia blouse

50
Moorish blanket

CONTENTS

Materials   4
Basic blackwork techniques   6

10

Tea light holders

14

Padded pouch

22

Embroidered garland

26

Pendant lampshade

30

Lace-look make-up bag

38

Black sampler

42

A fish on my satchel

46

Jolly table mats

54

Girl's dress

58

Elegant little mouse

MATERIALS

FOR EMBROIDERY

Blackwork is worked on embroidery canvas or evenweave cotton or linen with the same number of warp and weft threads per centimetre (or inch). The regular weave of these fabrics makes it easy to count threads for embroidery. For the projects in this book, I have mostly used 11 and 12 threads per cm (28 or 30 threads per inch).

Embroidery hoop

A hoop is useful for holding the fabric taut. It consists of two wooden hoops, one of which fits inside the other. Place the larger hoop with the adjustment screw on the table, lay the fabric on top of it and then insert the smaller hoop into the larger one. This will hold the fabric taut between the two hoops. Use the screw to adjust the fabric to the required tension. When embroidering, hold the hoop in one hand and use the other to bring the thread up and down through the fabric. In this book, we have used an embroidery hoop with a 12cm (4¾in) diameter.

Needles

The best needles to use are tapestry needles. They have blunt ends, which pass easily through the fabric. The size of the needle will depend on which fabric you are using; it should not force the threads of the fabric apart.
- For linen with 11 or 12 threads per cm (28 or 30 threads per inch), use size 26 needles.
- For sewing, use size 9 needles.

Thread

I have used three types of thread for the projects in this book: Retors du Nord embroidery floss, Calais Cocoon lace cotton thread and Caudry Cocoon lace cotton thread by Maison Sajou. These threads are widely available online. You can also use any other embroidery thread of your choice.
- Embroidery floss generally has six strands. I have used single or double thread to accentuate the thickness of certain designs.
- Calais Cocoon is ideal: this unique twisted, mercerized cotton is made up of three strands, it is flexible and slips easily through the fabric. It gives an even finish and makes it easy to embroider large patterns.
- Caudry Cocoon is a textured, gimped polyester thread with a metallic lurex strand. This thread should be used in shorter lengths.

Before starting to embroider, pull this thread through your fingers to ensure the two lengths are equal.

FOR SEWING

Certain tools are essential if you are going to do a good job.

- Thimble
- Sewing needles
- Pins
- Three pairs of scissors: fabric, embroidery and paper
- Erasable fabric pen
- 20cm (8in) ruler
- 50cm (20in) metal ruler
- Tacking/basting thread
- White, ecru and black sewing thread
- Iron-on fusible interfacing
- Quilt wadding (called batting in the US)
- Sewing machine
- Tracing paper or tissue paper
- Iron

> **Tip**
>
> *Keep a notebook and pencil close to hand to make notes while you are working on your projects.*

Difficulty levels

You will find these needle and thread symbols at the top of the first page of each project to give you an indication of the difficulty level.

𝓝	Very easy
𝓝𝓝	Easy
𝓝𝓝𝓝	More difficult

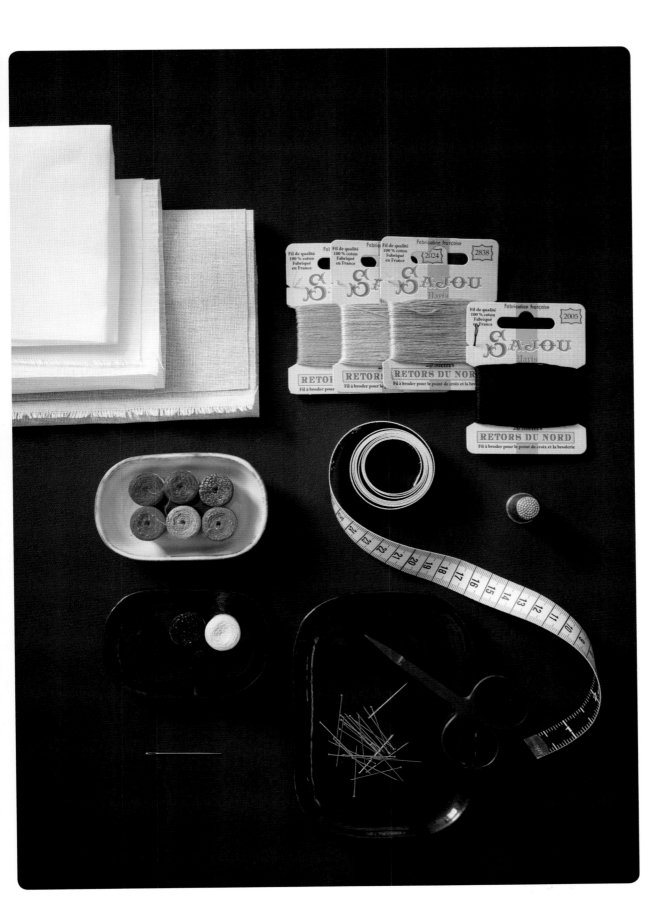

BASIC BLACKWORK TECHNIQUES

Blackwork is of Moorish origin and was introduced to the English court by Catherine of Aragon. Its defining feature is the repetition of geometric motifs embroidered in black, forming a patterned expanse of lines and arabesques. The complexity of the geometric designs gives a lace-like texture reminiscent of Moorish architecture.

STITCHES USED

Backstitch and Holbein stitch (or double running stitch) are the most commonly used stitches in blackwork.

Holbein stitch (or double running stitch)

This stitch is worked from right to left, counting the threads of the fabric.

1. Bring the needle up through the back of the fabric and then reinsert it two threads to the left, bring it up again a further two threads to the left and so on in the same way passing the thread over and under the threads of the fabric, following the line you are working.
2. Weave back in the opposite direction, filling in between the stitches worked previously, bringing the needle over and under the threads of the fabric to fill in the spaces in the line you are working. The threads of the fabric are no longer visible on the right side.

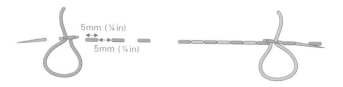

Backstitch

This stitch is used for outlining motifs and is worked from right to left.

1. Bring the needle up through the fabric at 1, then work a stitch to the right, passing the needle down at 2 on the line you are working. This will give you a horizontal stitch. Bring the needle back up to the left at 3, an equal distance from the previous stitch, and pull the length of thread through to the correct tension.
2. Work a backstitch by passing the needle back down at 2 and bringing it up at 3 at an equal distance from the previous stitches.
3. Continue, repeating step 2.

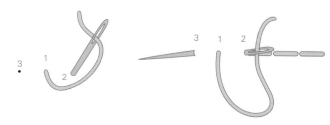

Stem stitch

This stitch is used for outlining motifs and is worked from left to right.

1. Bring the needle up through the fabric at 1, then work a slightly slanted stitch a few millimetres to the right, passing the needle down at 2 on the line of the design.
2. Bring the needle back up to the left at 3, halfway between points 1 and 2. Keep the thread to the bottom as you are working.
3. Continue in the same way, repeating the steps above.

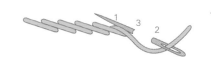

Chain stitch

This stitch is used for outlining motifs. It is worked from right to left or from top to bottom.

1. Bring the needle up through the fabric at 1, then reinsert the needle at the starting point and bring the point out a few millimetres to the left at 2. Pass the thread from left to right under the needle and pull the working thread through smoothly.
2. Work another stitch in the same way and of the same length to the left, inserting the needle at the base of the previous stitch where the stitch started and pulling the working thread through smoothly.
3. Continue in the same way, repeating steps 1 and 2.

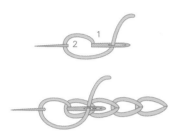

Lazy daisy stitch

This stitch is worked from top to bottom, like chain stitch.

1. Bring the needle up through the fabric at 1, then reinsert the needle in the same hole and bring it up the desired distance below at 2. Pass the thread from left to right under the needle and pull the working thread through smoothly.
2. Finish the stitch by making a small vertical stitch at the end of the loop formed in step 1, to anchor it in place.
3. Work another lazy daisy stitch, bringing the needle up at the desired point and repeating steps 1 and 2.

Catch stitch

Similar to herringbone stitch, this stitch holds hems and wadding/batting in place during sewing. It is worked from left to right and from bottom to top on two parallel lines.

1. Bring the needle up through the fabric at 1 and work a stitch diagonally to the right at 2. Bring the needle up again to left at 3 on the same horizontal line. You have created a diagonal stitch to the right.
2. Work a stitch diagonally to the lower right at 4, reinserting on the same horizontal line as the starting point, and come up again at 5 on the same line. You have created a second diagonal stitch which crosses the first.
3. Continue, repeating steps 1 and 2, and finish with a diagonal half-stitch.

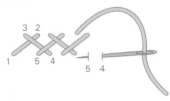

Straight stitch

This stitch is used to form a long, straight stitch either individually, or in groups to form patterns.

1. Bring the needle up through the fabric at 1 and reinsert above at 2, then bring the needle up a few millimetres to the right of the second stitch at 3.
2. Repeat step 1 to work the other stitches.

These stitches can be vertical, horizontal or diagonal, short or long. More than one straight stitch can be worked from the same starting point.

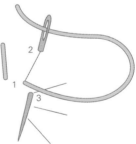

Satin stitch

These stitches can be vertical, horizontal or diagonal and can get longer or shorter.

1. Bring the needle up through the fabric at 1 and reinsert above at 2, then bring the needle up on the same line at 3, just to the right of the previous stitch.
2. Repeat this stage to work the other stitches to the desired length.

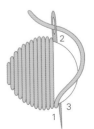

Wrapped running stitch

This stitch is worked from right to left.
1. Bring the needle up through the fabric at 1, then work a small stitch to the left on the line that you are working, bringing the needle back up at 2. This will give you a horizontal stitch. Bring the needle back up to the left at 3, a few threads further on, and pull the working thread through smoothly. Continue along the line you are working.
2. Working on the stitches that you have just created, bring the needle up through the fabric under the first stitch and pass it under each stitch made in step 1 by sliding the needle from top to bottom under each stitch. In this way you create a series of wrapped stitches with a slight wave.

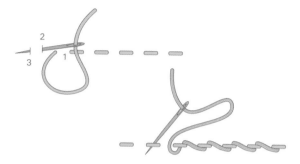

Fly stitch

This stitch is like an open lazy daisy stitch. In this book, it is worked at an acute angle. It is worked from left to right.
1. Bring the needle up through the fabric at 1 and, keeping the thread to the bottom, reinsert the needle at point 2 to the right (the distance will depend on the desired effect). Bring it out further down at 3, at the desired distance, midway between points 1 and 2.
2. Finish the stitch by making a small vertical stitch over the end of the curve formed to anchor the stitch in place (4).
3. Work another stitch by bringing the needle up at the desired point and repeating the previous steps.

French knot

In this book, this stitch is used to create the centre of flowers.
1. Bring the needle up through the fabric at 1 and wrap the thread around the needle. Reinsert the needle at 2 inside the loop, one or two weft threads from the starting point.
2. Pull the working thread through smoothly, while also pulling on the base of the thread to hold the loop tight around the needle against the fabric.
3. Pull the working thread all the way through, still keeping the wrapped loop tight, until it has all passed through the knot you have formed. Be very careful not to pull the working thread too tight at the end, as you may pull the knot through to the underside of the fabric.

DRAWN THREAD EMBROIDERY

Making the open areas for drawn thread embroidery requires preparation: remove the weft threads to the desired height and length to obtain a network of threads known as the 'barelaid warp', which you will use as a base for your work.
1. Define the height and length of the work by counting the warp and weft threads.
2. Use a round-tipped needle to lift the thread in the middle of the defined space, then cut it in the middle with some fine-pointed scissors.
3. Draw out the thread on either side to the defined limit, without cutting further, by lifting and pulling them with the needle. Gradually draw out all the required threads to create an open area of barelaid warp threads (A).
4. On either side of the open area, work the drawn threads in on the wrong side: thread each thread through the needle and weave into the backing fabric for 1 to 3cm (½ to 1¼in) depending on the project, then cut off the tail flat against the back of the work. This work will be hidden in the hem (B).

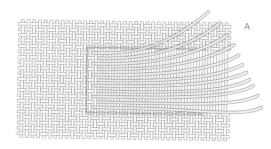

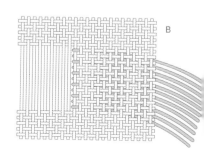

Hem stitch

Work over a number of threads that is a multiple of three, following the explanations below to obtain three-thread bundles.

1. Once you have bared the warp threads, you are going to sew them into bundles, working hem stitch along the bottom edge of the wrong side of the open area, from left to right. Anchor the thread by oversewing vertically adjacent to the open area, leaving a tail of around 8cm (3¼in).
2. Work a small vertical stitch on the edge to the left of the first bundle, slide the needle from right to left, behind the chosen number of vertical threads, and pull the needle through smoothly to draw the base together (A).
3. Reinsert the needle vertically from the back to the front, to the right of the first bundle, bringing it out two threads of fabric below the edge of the open area.
4. Repeat these stages along the full length, finishing with the thread at the back. Work in the tail by sliding the needle under the last few stitches. Undo the oversewing used to anchor the thread at the starting point and work in the tail under the first few stitches. Repeat the process on the opposite edge working on the wrong side, from left to right (C).

Mitred corners

1. Finish the edges of the fabric and prepare each side in turn. Fold in the seam allowance, marking the fold with an iron, then open out again before preparing the next side (1).
2. Fold in each of the corners diagonally, lining up the fold lines. Press in the fold with an iron. Open out the corners again and draw a parallel line 1.5cm (⅝in) outside the diagonal fold. Cut the fabric along this line (2).
3. Fold the fabric diagonally, right sides together, and sew along the diagonal corner fold, from the outside to the inside, starting the seam 1cm (⅜in) from the edge (3). Trim the corners, turn the hem the right way out and push out the corners using a leadless pencil. Iron the edges carefully.
4. Turn the edges of the seam allowance under 1cm (⅜in) around the inside edge. The corners are easy to position as long as you have not sewn right to the edge (if you have, unpick slightly) (4).
5. Pin into place, tack/baste and sew the hem using invisible stitches or catch stitch (5).

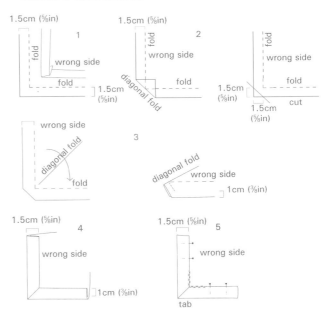

Finishing embroidery

Here are a few tips to achieve a perfect finish for your embroidery.

Once you have finished embroidering, work in the tails of the threads by weaving them through the underside of the stitches. Wash your work carefully using household soap. Leave to dry flat and press with an iron while still damp on the wrong side of the embroidery on top of a towel.

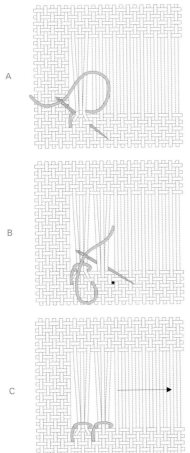

9

TEA LIGHT HOLDERS

Openwork embroidery and blackwork lace to create an eye-catching glow.

MATERIALS

* White linen fabric, 12 threads/cm (30 threads/in): three pieces 30 x 10cm (11¾ x 4in)
* Caudry cocoon black (3180) and red (3434) thread, 1 cocoon of each

SIZE OF FINISHED MODEL

5 x 6cm (2 x 2⅜in)

EMBROIDERY SIZE

Approximately 20.5 x 4.3cm (8 x 1¾in)

STITCHES USED

Holbein stitch
Drawn thread stitches:
hem stitch, zigzag and knotted

DRAWN THREAD BACKGROUND

1. Finish the edges of the three linen rectangles.
2. Create the drawn thread backgrounds on each rectangle following the instructions on page 8.
3. Mark the centre of the fabric by tacking/basting vertically up the middle. Check the size of the open area of drawn threads with reference to the relevant chart, working on the wrong side.

Tip

You can adapt the embroidery to other sizes of tea lights by adjusting the number of times you work the repeat.

Design 1 – Hem stitch

1. Withdraw 16 threads and weave the ends in to the 1.5cm (⅝in) hem area on each side (see diagrams A and B on page 8).
2. Use hem stitch to create simple bundles of threads, from left to right, using the red thread. Work along the bottom edge of the open area, then the upper edge. Each bundle should consist of three threads, resulting in a total of 82 bundles (see diagrams A, B and C on page 9).

Design 1

Repeat 7 x 4 squares

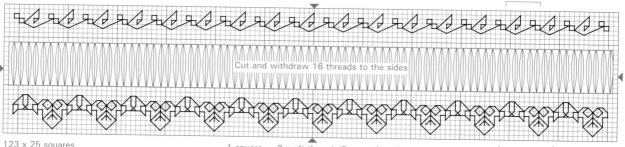

Cut and withdraw 16 threads to the sides

1 square = 2 weft threads/2 warp threads

123 x 25 squares
Embroidered area: 20.5 x 4.1cm (8 x 1⅝in)
Upper strip: 121 x 4 squares/20.1 x 0.7cm (7¾ x ¼in)
Lower strip: 121 x 7 squares/20.1 x 1.1cm (7¾ x ½in)
Dimension of open area: 21 x 1.3cm (8¼ x ½in)

Repeat 11 x 7 squares

Caudry cocoon
—— Black 3180: 1 thread, backstitch
—— Red 3434: 1 thread, hem stitch

Design 2 – Coral knots

1. Withdraw 16 threads and weave the ends in to the 1.5cm (⅝in) hem area on each side. Work on the wrong side from left to right, using the red thread.

2. Prepare bundles of two threads each, following the instructions for hem stitching. You now have 122 bundles of two threads.

3. Knot two bundles together: insert the needle halfway up, oversewing to the side to anchor your thread. With the thread in front, knot two bundles together: pass the needle from right to left behind two bundles, bring the thread back over the bundles and pass it through the loop of thread. Pull the working thread through, forming a knot around the bundles that are now pulled together. Continue in the same way, ensuring there is even thread tension between the knotted bundles. You should end up with 61 knotted bundles.

Design 3 – Zigzag hem stitch

1. Withdraw 15 threads and weave the ends in to the 1.5cm (⅝in) hem area on each side. Work on the wrong side, using the red thread. Prepare bundles of four threads each, following the instructions for hem stitching.

2. Working from right to left, work one bundle of two threads, and then continue making bundles of four threads. Work along the upper edge of the open area in the same way. You will end up with 61 bundles of four threads with a bundle of two threads at the start of each edge.

Design 2

Repeat 8 x 4 squares

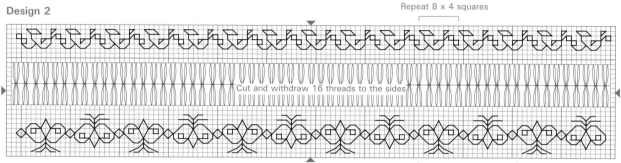

Cut and withdraw 16 threads to the sides

Repeat 20 x 8 squares

122 x 26 squares
Embroidered area: 20.3 x 4.1cm (8 x 1⅝in)
Upper strip: 121 x 4 squares/20.1 x 0.7cm (7¾ x ¼in)
Lower strip: 120 x 8 squares/20 x 1cm (7¾ x ⅜in)
Dimension of open area: 20.3 x 1.5cm (8 x ⅝in)

1 square = 2 weft threads/
2 warp threads

Caudry cocoon
— Black 3180: 1 thread, backstitch
— Red 3434: 1 thread, coral knots

Design 3

Repeat 12 x 8 squares

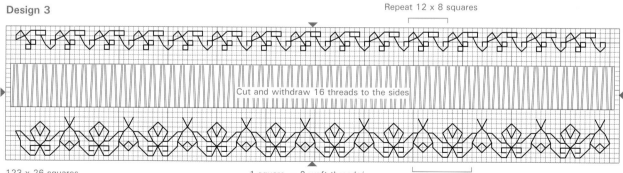

Cut and withdraw 16 threads to the sides

Repeat 11 x 7 squares

123 x 26 squares
Embroidered area: 20.5 x 4.3cm (8 x 1⅝in)
Upper strip: 120 x 4 squares/20 x 0.7cm (7¾ x ¼in)
Lower strip: 121 x 8 squares/20.1 x 1cm (7¾ x ⅜in)
Dimension of open area: 20.3 x 1.5cm (8 x ⅝in)

1 square = 2 weft threads/
2 warp threads

Caudry cocoon
— Black 3180: 1 thread, backstitch
— Red 3434: 1 thread, coral knots

EMBROIDERY

1. Embroider the upper and lower band with Holbein stitch, working from the centre, following the diagrams. The upper bands are embroidered six threads above the band of drawn thread work, the lower bands, four threads below the rectangle of drawn thread work.
2. Finish following the instructions on page 9.

MAKING UP

1. Fold in half widthways, right sides together, sew together 1cm (⅜in) from the end of the rectangle of drawn thread work.
2. Press the seam open with an iron and trim seam allowance to 2cm (¾in). Turn in a further 1cm (⅜in) of each stitch allowance, press, and sew into place using invisible stitches (1).

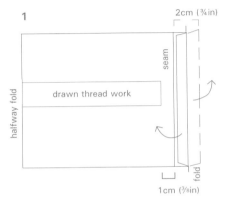

1

halfway fold

drawn thread work

seam

2cm (¾in)

fold

1cm (⅜in)

3. Repeat this process on the band under the drawn thread work, making the first fold 1cm (⅜in) above the narrower embroidered band. Sew the hem into place with invisible stitches. Turn the right way out (3).

FINISHING

1. Create a double fold hem above the edge of the wider embroidered band by folding the fabric to the wrong side, 0.5cm (¼in) from the embroidery and pressing the fold into place with an iron. Then turn the hem in again to just above the drawn thread work. Press the fold with an iron and sew into place using invisible stitches (2).
2. Repeat this process on the band under the drawn thread work, making the first fold 1cm (⅜in) above the narrower embroidered band. Sew the hem into place with invisible stitches. Turn the right way out (3).

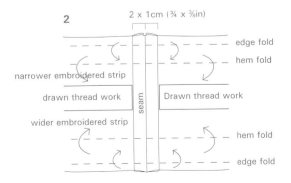

2

2 x 1cm (¾ x ⅜in)

edge fold

hem fold

narrower embroidered strip

drawn thread work

seam

Drawn thread work

wider embroidered strip

hem fold

edge fold

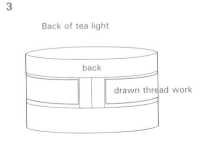

3

Back of tea light

back

drawn thread work

PADDED POUCH

A great interplay of pattern and colour is created by the chequerboard effect of the fabric and the finely embroidered flap.

MATERIALS

* White linen fabric, 12 threads/cm (30 threads/in): 20 x 45cm (7¾ x 17¾in)
* Black/ecru check fabric: 18.5 x 32cm (7¼ x 12½in)
* Wadding/batting: 16.5 x 30cm (6½ x 11¾in)
* Retors du Nord black (2005) thread: 1 card
* Sewing and embroidery equipment

FINISHED SIZE

16 x 14cm (6¼ x 5½in)

SIZE OF EMBROIDERED FLAP

14.5 x 3.5cm (5¾ x 1⅜in)

STITCHES USED

Holbein stitch

Catch stitch

EMBROIDERY (diagram on page 16)

1. From the white linen, cut: 1 piece A measuring 18.5 x 30cm (7¼ x 11¾in) and 1 piece C measuring 18.5 x 14cm (7¼ x 5½in). Use a sewing machine to finish the raw edges.
2. Mark where the embroidery will start on part A by tacking/basting vertically up the middle for 8cm (3¼in). Then tack/baste a horizontal line 2cm (¾in) from the bottom (see diagram 1).
3. Work on an embroidery frame. Start embroidering in the middle at the bottom of the diagram, setting off from the point at the centre where the two lines of tacking/basting cross. Embroider in Holbein stitch using one or two strands of thread.
4. Finish by following the instructions on page 9.

Tip

To ensure you follow the grain of the fabric, tack/baste along all reference lines.

PREPARATION

The pouch is made up of three pieces.
* The embroidered base of piece A: the lower part of the flap, with the remaining part forming the lining of the flap and the back.
* Piece B (patterned fabric): outside of the pouch.
* Piece C: lining of the front of the pouch.

Work on the right side of piece A across the width.

1. Tack/baste a first line 1cm (⅜in) above the embroidery to mark the seamline of where piece A will be joined to piece B (1). Tack/baste a second line 8.5cm (3¼in) above the first to mark the top fold of the flap. Tack/baste a third line 14cm (5½in) above that to mark the seamline at the bottom of the lining where the work will be closed up (1).
2. On the wrong side of piece B, define the area to be padded by drawing a line 1cm (⅜in) from each side; this will give you a 16.5 x 30cm (6½ x 11¾in) rectangle. Centre the wadding/batting, tack/baste and sew it to the edges of the fabric using catch stitch, catching the fabric and wadding/batting alternately (2).

1

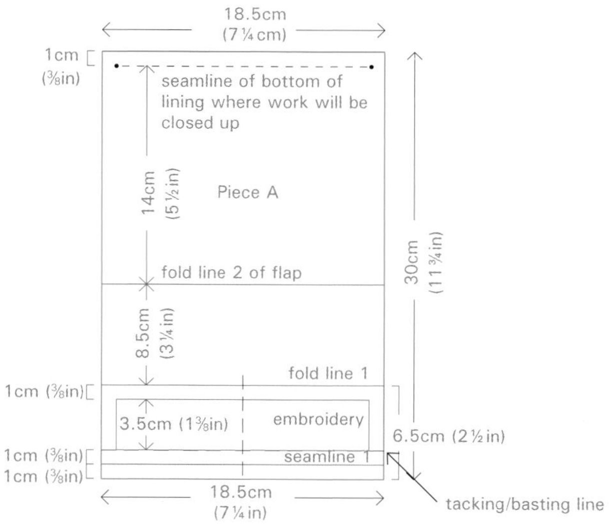

18.5cm (7¼ cm)

1cm (⅜in)

seamline of bottom of lining where work will be closed up

14cm (5½in)

Piece A

fold line 2 of flap

8.5cm (3¼in)

fold line 1

1cm (⅜in)

3.5cm (1⅜in)   embroidery

1cm (⅜in)
1cm (⅜in)

seamline 1

6.5cm (2½in)

18.5cm (7¼in)

tacking/basting line

30cm (11¾in)

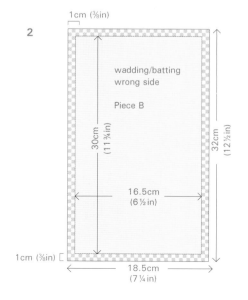

2

1cm (⅜in)

wadding/batting wrong side

Piece B

30cm (11¾in)

32cm (12½in)

16.5cm (6½in)

1cm (⅜in)

18.5cm (7¼in)

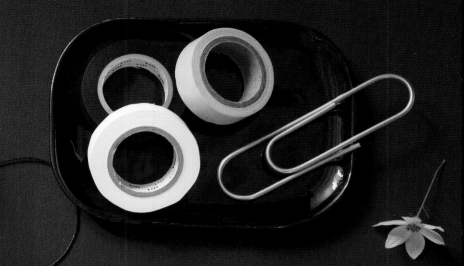

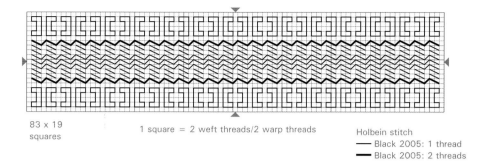

83 x 19 squares

1 square = 2 weft threads/2 warp threads

Holbein stitch
—— Black 2005: 1 thread
━━ Black 2005: 2 threads

ASSEMBLY

Tip

Use the lines you tacked/basted earlier on piece A to help make up the pouch.

1. Place piece A right side up with the embroidery at the top.
2. Place piece B on the embroidery, right sides together, pin in place and sew along the width, 1cm (⅜in) from the edge along the first seamline (3 – seamline 1). Unfold into a strip and press open the seams with an iron.
3. Fold piece A at fold line 1 (4), folding it against the right side of piece B. This will hide the embroidery and forms the fold at the base of the flap.
4. Working on the wrong side, pin together and sew side seams 1cm (⅜in) from the edges, stopping 2cm (¾in) below the flap fold line of piece A. Fold the part of piece A that has not been seamed upwards and secure out of the way with a pin.
5. Place piece C on the bottom of piece B, right sides together; pin and sew along seamline 2 (4 and 5). Press the seams open with an iron.
6. Fold piece B right sides together, placing the last seam sewn (seamline 2) against the fold formed in piece A previously. Now piece B is folded right sides together, with the wadded part on the outside. Fold piece C up to the top of the work. Sew up each side 1cm (⅜in) from the edge, from the bottom fold of the pouch to the seam joining pieces A and B.
7. Take the part of piece A that was pinned up and piece C which makes up the lining (6). Fold the parts that have already been sewn and that form the body of the pouch to one side to make it easier to work. Lay A on top of C, pin into place, and sew along each side 1cm (⅜in) from the edge, starting from the seam allowances of the parts already made up (6). Open out the seams, trim the corners slightly, fold a 1cm (⅜in) seam allowance along the remaining open edge, and mark the fold with an iron.
8. Turn the pouch the right way out: start with the embroidered part, then the front, and push out the corners.

3

right side piece A
18.5cm (7¼in)
fold line 1

right side embroidery
seamline 1
5.5cm (2¼in)

32cm (12½in)

right side piece B

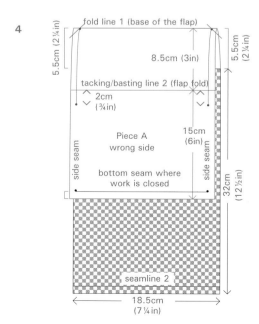

4

fold line 1 (base of the flap)
5.5cm (2¼in)
8.5cm (3in)
5.5cm (2¼in)

tacking/basting line 2 (flap fold)
2cm (¾in)

Piece A
wrong side

15cm (6in)

side seam
side seam

bottom seam where work is closed

32cm (12½in)

seamline 2

18.5cm (7¼in)

FINISHING

Sew up the bottom seam of the lining, turning in the 1cm (⅜in) seam allowance of pieces A and C. Sew up with invisible stitches, catching each piece with the needle in turn.

> **Tip**
>
> *Replace the chequerboard fabric with black for a chic look or go sophisticated by using white.*

5

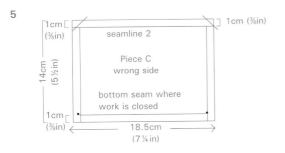

1cm (⅜in)

seamline 2

Piece C
wrong side

bottom seam where
work is closed

1cm (⅜in)

14cm (5½in)

18.5cm (7¼in)

6

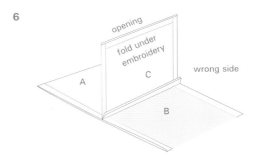

opening

fold under
embroidery

A   C

B

wrong side

Finished pouch

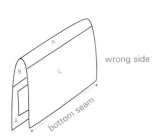

A

B   C

A

wrong side

bottom seam

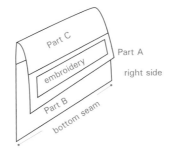

Part C

embroidery

Part B

Part A

right side

bottom seam

17

MOTH-PATTERNED PILLOWS

Lace moths take flight and forage on these blue pillows.

MATERIALS

SQUARE PILLOW

* Raw linen fabric, 12 threads/cm (30 threads/in): 27 x 30cm (10¾ x 11¾in)
* Thin interfacing: 22.5 x 19.5cm (8⅞ x 7⅝in)
* Retors du Nord black (2005) thread: 1 card
* Calais Cocoon black (6118) thread: 1 cocoon
* Caudry Cocoon black (3180) thread: 1 cocoon
* Square pillow: 40 x 40cm (15¾ x 15¾in)
* Sewing and embroidery equipment

RECTANGULAR PILLOW

* Raw linen, 12 threads/cm (30 threads/in): 27 x 33cm (10¾ x 13in)
* Raw cotton lining: 18.5 x 33cm (7¼ x 13in)
* Thin interfacing: 19.5 x 33cm (7⅝ x 13in)
* Retors du Nord black (2005) thread: 1 card
* Calais Cocoon black (6118) thread: 1 cocoon
* Caudry Cocoon black (3180) thread: 1 cocoon
* Rectangular pillow 50 x 30cm (19¾ x 11¾in)
* Sewing and embroidery equipment

FINISHED SIZE

Square pillow: 40 x 40cm (15¾ x 15¾in)
Rectangular pillow: 50 x 30cm (19¾ x 11¾in)

EMBROIDERY SIZE

Square pillow: 20.5 x 17.5cm (8 x 6⅞in)
Rectangular pillow: 17.5 x 20.5cm (6⅞ x 8in)

STITCHES USED

Holbein stitch
Catch stitch
Backstitch

EMBROIDERY (diagrams on pages 20 and 21)

1. Mark the centre of your fabric, both horizontally and vertically, with tacking/basting stitches. Find the centre of the diagram by following the arrows on each side. Embroider from the centre of the fabric using Holbein stitch with one or two threads.
2. Finish following the instructions on page 9.

MAKING UP

Square pillow (see diagrams below)

1. Working on the right side of piece A, draw cutting lines 2cm (¾in) from each side of the embroidery. Cut out the fabric along these lines to obtain a 24.5 x 21.5cm (9⅝ x 8½in) rectangle. Finish the edges (1).
2. On the wrong side of piece A, define the area to be interfaced by drawing a line 1cm (⅜in) from each edge of the embroidery.

Fold along these lines following the grain of the fabric to obtain a 22.5 x 19.5cm (8⅞ x 7⅝in) rectangle. Place piece B of the interfacing (22.5 x 19.5cm (8⅞ x 7⅝in)) with the glued side against the wrong side of the centred embroidery, in the space formed by the folds. Tack/baste into place and iron on (2).
3. Turn in the edges following the grain of the fabric, form the corners (see page 9) and iron on the wrong side. You now have a 22.5 x 19.5cm (8⅞ x 7⅝in) rectangle (3). Sew around the edges using catch stitch.
4. Centre the embroidery on the pillow, pin and tack/baste to hold in place.
5. Sew all round the embroidered piece using invisible stitches, catching each of the two fabrics with the needle in turn.

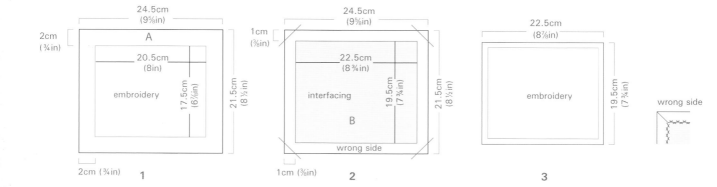

Rectangular pillow (see diagrams opposite)

1. Working on the right side of piece A, with a height of 33cm (13in), draw cutting lines 2cm (¾in) from each side of the embroidery. Cut out the fabric along these lines to obtain a 21.5 x 33cm (8½ x 13in) rectangle and finish the edges (1).

2. On the wrong side of piece A, define the area to be interfaced by drawing a line 1cm (⅜in) from each side of the rectangle. Fold along these lines following the grain of the fabric to obtain a 19.5 x 33cm (7⅝ x 13in) rectangle. Place piece B of the interfacing (19.5 x 33cm (7⅝ x 13in)) with the glued side against the wrong side of the embroidery, in the space formed by the folds. Tack/baste into place and iron on (2).

3. Line the rectangle with the 18.5 x 33cm (7¼ x 13in) piece of raw cotton (piece C) and finish the edges.

4. Place the lining and the embroidery right sides together lined up down one side, pin and sew 0.5cm (¼in) from the edge. Press open the seam with an iron. Do the same up the other side. Turn the right way out and iron, centring the lining: you now have a 19.5cm (7⅝in) wide rectangle, with a 0.5cm (¼in) border on each side formed from piece A (3). Turn in 1cm (⅜in) at the top and bottom of the rectangle between the two thicknesses of fabric and close the openings with invisible stitches.

5. Centre rectangle C on the pillow, right side of the embroidery up, pin at the top and bottom and tack/baste to hold in place.

6. Sew on the embroidered rectangle using invisible stitches along the top and bottom seams of the pillow.

Square pillow

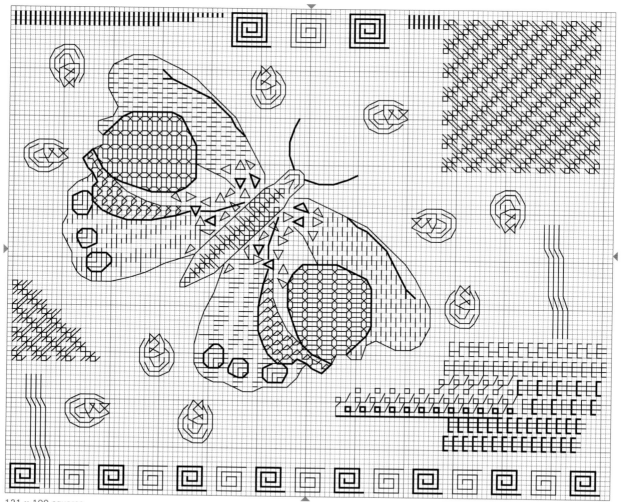

121 x 100 squares

1 square = 2 weft threads/2 warp threads

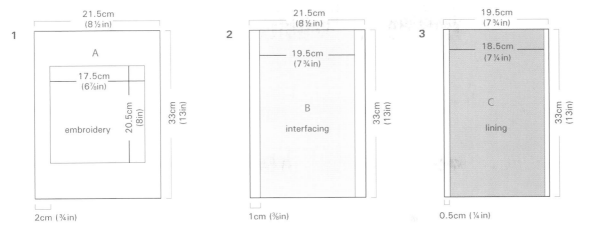

1

21.5cm
(8½in)

A

17.5cm
(6⅞in)

20.5cm
(8in)

33cm
(13in)

embroidery

2cm (¾in)

2

21.5cm
(8½in)

19.5cm
(7¾in)

B

interfacing

33cm
(13in)

1cm (⅜in)

3

19.5cm
(7¾in)

18.5cm
(7¼in)

C

lining

33cm
(13in)

0.5cm (¼in)

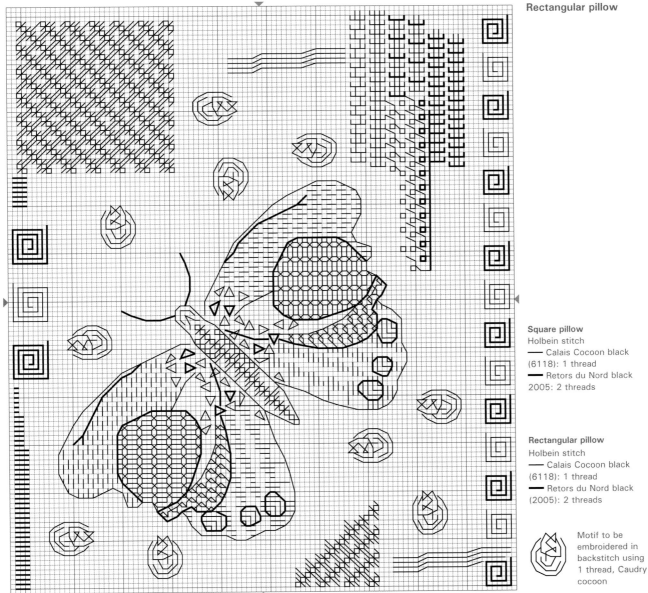

Rectangular pillow

100 x 121 squares

1 square = 2 weft threads/2 warp threads

Square pillow
Holbein stitch
— Calais Cocoon black
(6118): 1 thread
— Retors du Nord black
2005: 2 threads

Rectangular pillow
Holbein stitch
— Calais Cocoon black
(6118): 1 thread
— Retors du Nord black
(2005): 2 threads

Motif to be
embroidered in
backstitch using
1 thread, Caudry
cocoon

21

EMBROIDERED GARLAND

All you need is a length of linen yarn, a few buttons and some embroidered mini-pillows to create this pretty bunting.

MATERIALS

* Off-white linen fabric, 12 threads/cm (30 threads/in): 45 x 45cm (17¾ x 17¾in)
* Retors du Nord black (6180) thread: 1 card
* 2m (79in) of white linen yarn
* Seven mother-of-pearl buttons (old or new), 2cm (¾in) in diameter
* Toy stuffing
* Sewing and embroidery equipment

FINISHED SIZE

The garland measures 40cm (15¾in)
Each pillow measures 8.5 x 8.5cm (3⅜ x 3⅜in)

EMBROIDERY SIZE

Approximately 5.5 x 5.5cm (2¼ x 2¼in)

STITCHES USED

Holbein stitch

EMBROIDERY (diagrams on pages 24 and 25)

1. Cut eight 16 x 16cm (6¼ x 6¼in) squares from the linen and finish the edges.
2. Mark the centre of the fabric with tacking/basting stitches. Find the centre of the diagram by following the arrows on each side.
3. Embroider using Holbein stitch from the centre of the fabric, following the diagram.
4. Finish following the instructions on page 9.

MAKING UP

Prepare each square in the same way.

1. Working on the right side, draw cutting lines 1.5cm (⅝in) from each side of the embroidery. Cut out the fabric along these lines to obtain a 10.5 x 10.5cm (4⅛ x 4⅛in) rectangle. Finish the edges. Cut out an identical eight squares for the backs of the pillows.
2. Lay the back and the front of the pillow right sides together (embroidery inside), and pin to hold in place. Sew round three sides, 1cm (⅜in) from the edge, leaving one side open. Trim the corners, press open the seams with an iron and turn the right way out, ensuring that each corner is properly formed. Stuff lightly, turn in a 1cm (⅜in) seam allowance along the opening, and sew up using invisible stitches. Repeat for the other seven mini-pillows. Steam-iron lightly.

FINISHING

1. Thread the needle with the linen yarn, leaving a tail of around 45cm (17¾in) at the start. Make a knot on the back edge of one of the pillows, then sew four long straight stitches along the top of the back, finishing with a knot on the opposite side to secure.
2. Pass the working yarn through the holes of the first button, and slide it along the thread to a distance of around 3cm (1¼in) from the pillow. Continue attaching the other pillows and buttons, spacing them all 3cm (1¼in) apart.
3. Leaving a 45cm (17¾in) length of yarn, finish with a loop at each end so you can hang the garland up.

> **Tip**
>
> *The embroidered areas on the different pillows are of slightly different sizes. The central tacking/basting line means you can centre the embroidery to obtain pillows of the same size.*

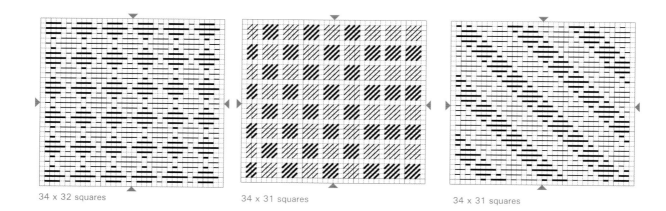

34 x 32 squares

34 x 31 squares

34 x 31 squares

31 x 32 squares

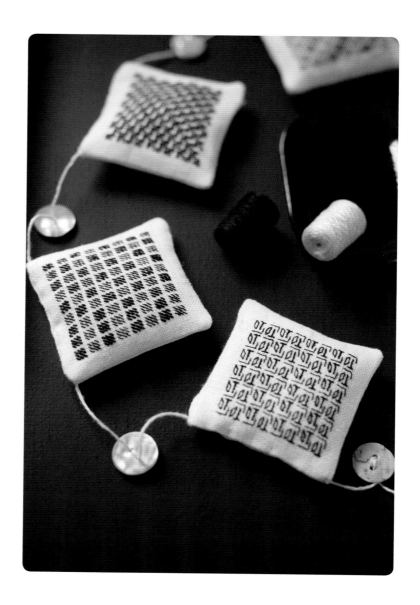

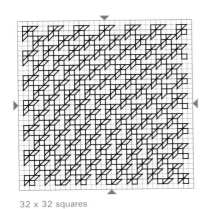

32 x 32 squares

31 x 32 squares

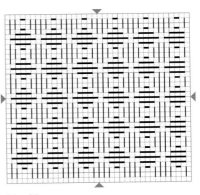

34 x 32 squares

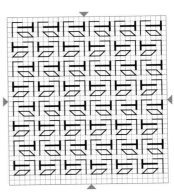

29 x 31 squares

1 square = 2 weft threads/2 warp threads

Size of squares
5.3 x 5.3cm (2 x 2in)
5.6 x 5.1cm (2 ¼ x 1 ⅞in)
5.6 x 5.3cm (2 ¼ x 2in)

Retors du Nord black 2005
—— 1 thread
▬▬ 2 threads

PENDANT LAMPSHADE

Graphic motifs and a repeated border pattern create a chic, decorative lampshade.

MATERIALS

* White linen fabric, 12 threads/cm (30 threads/in): 100 x 40cm (39⅜ x 16in)
* White tarlatan fabric: 81.5 x 25cm (32 x 9¾in)
* Calais Cocoon black (6180) thread: 3 cocoons
* Retors du Nord black (2005) thread: 2 cards
* Two white lampshade rings, 25cm (9¾in) in diameter, one with a spider fitting
* Sewing and embroidery equipment

FINISHED SIZE

Diameter 25cm (9¾in); height 24cm (9½in)

EMBROIDERY SIZE

78.5 x 19cm (31 x 7½in)

STITCHES USED

Holbein stitch
Backstitch

EMBROIDERY (diagrams on page 29)

1. Finish the edges of the linen.
2. Tack/baste three lines along the full width:
   * Line 1: halfway up
   * Line 2: 5.6cm (2¼in) above the central line
   * Line 3: 5.6cm (2¼in) below the central line
3. Tack/baste a vertical line from top to bottom to mark the centre. The central line will act as a basis for embroidering the central motifs; the other two lines mark the bases of the embroidered border patterns.
4. Locate the centre of the diagram by following the arrows on each side. Embroider around the middle of the linen using the diagram of the central part of the lampshade and the central tacked/basted line as reference. Embroider the border patterns using the relevant diagrams and tacked/basted lines 2 and 3 as reference, starting with the upper border.
5. Finish the embroidery following the instructions on page 9.

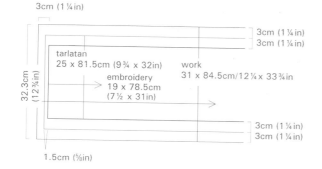

MAKING UP

1. Work on the right side of the embroidery. Draw cutting lines along the 78.5cm (31in) length, 6cm (2⅜in) from the embroidery. Draw cutting lines along each vertical side 3cm (1¼in) from the embroidery.
2. Cut the fabric along these lines. Now you have a 31 x 84.5cm (12¼ x 33¼in) rectangle. Finish the edges.
3. On the wrong side, define the area to be lined with the tarlatan by drawing parallel lines 3cm (1¼in) above and below the embroidery and 1cm (⅜in) on each side. Fold the fabric along the grain on these lines, and press each fold to the wrong side with an iron.
4. Centre the 25 x 81.5cm (9¾ x 32in) rectangle of tarlatan in the space marked by the folds made above (extending 1.5cm (⅝in) at the top and bottom) and tack/baste to secure in place.
5. Fold the strip in two widthways, right sides together, embroidery inwards. Line up the top edges and ensure that the border patterns are aligned at the ends, then pin and tack/baste to secure. Sew from top to bottom. You now have a cylinder. Press the seams open with an iron and secure the tarlatan with invisible stitches around each side.
6. Working on the wrong side, fold the edges down 3cm (1¼in) at the top and bottom, following the grain of the fabric; iron on the wrong side to press the folds and secure with pins. Turn the edge in a further 1.5cm (⅝in) to create a double hem.

FINISHING

1. Place the ring with the spider fitting inside the cylinder, inside the seam fold (spider fitter downwards), then fold the 1.5cm (⅝in) hem over the ring. Press the fold into place following the grain of the fabric and pin to secure. Tack/baste and use invisible stitches to secure.
2. Attach the lower ring in the same way.

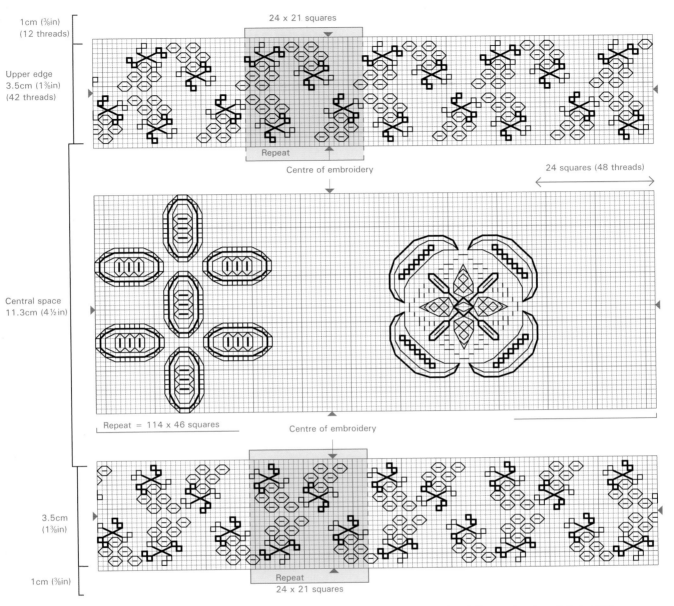

24 x 21 squares

Repeat

Centre of embroidery

24 squares (48 threads)

1cm (⅜in)
(12 threads)

Upper edge
3.5cm (1⅜in)
(42 threads)

Centre of embroidery

Repeat = 114 x 46 squares

Central space
11.3cm (4½in)

3.5cm
(1⅜in)

1cm (⅜in)

Repeat
24 x 21 squares

Embroidered area: 456 x 110 squares
Width: 78.5cm (31in); height: 20.3cm (8in)

1 square = 2 weft threads/2 warp threads

Holbein stitch
Calais Cocoon black (6180)
—— 1 threads

Backstitch
Retors du Nord black (2005)
—— 2 threads

Tip

The tacking/basting lines are essential. The horizontal lines help you to position the motifs. The vertical lines show where you start embroidering and the border pattern repeats.

LACE-LOOK MAKE-UP BAG

This richly embroidered bag is sure to attract envious glances.

MATERIALS

* White linen fabric, 12 threads/cm (30 threads/in): 26 x 21cm (10¼ x 8¼in)
* White silk fabric: 26 x 21cm (10¼ x 8¼in)
* Patterned cotton fabric: 26 x 21cm (20½ x 8¼in)
* Wadding/batting: 24 x 17.5cm (9½ x 6⅞in)
* Retors du Nord black (2005) thread: 2 cards
* Matching invisible zip fastener: 23cm (9in)
* Sewing and embroidery equipment

FINISHED SIZE

24 x 18.5cm (9½ x 7¼in)

EMBROIDERY SIZE

22 x 15cm (8¾ x 6in)

STITCHES USED

Holbein stitch
Catch stitch

EMBROIDERY (diagram on page 33)

1. Finish the edges of the linen.
2. Find the centre of the diagram by following the arrows on each side. Embroider from the centre of the fabric using Holbein stitch.
3. Finish following the instructions on page 9.

> **Tip**
>
> *This combination of embroidered motifs requires careful attention, but the result is worth the effort.*

1

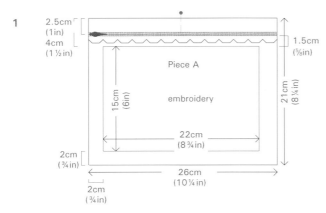

2.5cm (1in)
4cm (1½in)
1.5cm (⅝in)

Piece A

embroidery

15cm (6in)
21cm (8¼in)
22cm (8¾in)

2cm (¾in)
26cm (10¼in)
2cm (¾in)

2

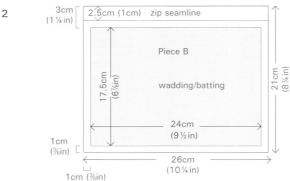

3cm (1¼in)   2.5cm (1cm)   zip seamline

Piece B

wadding/batting

17.5cm (6⅞in)
21cm (8¼in)
24cm (9½in)

1cm (⅜in)
26cm (10¼in)
1cm (⅜in)

3

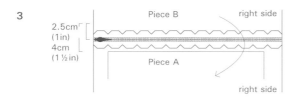

Piece B   right side

2.5cm (1in)
4cm (1½in)

Piece A

right side

MAKING UP

1. Working on the right side of the embroidery (piece A), mark a line 2.5cm (1in) from the top by folding the fabric to the wrong side and pressing with an iron. Open out the fold and mark the centre by inserting a pin perpendicular to the edge.
2. Centre the zip, placing the edges of the zip along the fold, secure in place by tacking/basting along the fold line. Open out the fold again, and sew along the zip on the machine using the appropriate zipper foot. Press the seam to the wrong side of piece A.
3. On the wrong side of silk piece B, define the area to pad by drawing a vertical line 3cm (1¼in) from the edge (zip side), then three other lines 1cm (⅜in) from the edge on the remaining sides. You now have a 24 x 17.5cm (9½ x 6⅞in) rectangle.
4. Centre the wadding/batting on top, tack/baste along the top to hold in place, then catch stitch round the sides and the bottom, alternately catching the silk and the wadding/batting with the needle.
5. Working on the right side of piece B, mark a line 2.5cm (1in) from the top by folding the fabric to the wrong side and pressing with an iron. Open out the fold and mark the centre by inserting a pin. Sew up the other side of the zip as previously.

ASSEMBLY

> **Tip**
>
> *During the final stages, do not forget to open the zip a third of the way so you can turn the work the right way out.*

1. Fold piece B over piece A, right sides together, with the zip at the top.
2. Sew up each side on the machine, 1cm (⅜in) from the edge, remembering to open the zip before sewing the third seam. Iron open the seams, and trim the corners.
3. Make the lining from piece C (patterned cotton), 52 x 21cm (20½ x 8¼in). Fold in half the top to the bottom, right sides together; pin the sides and sew them up 1cm (⅜in) from the edge. Iron open the seams, and trim the corners.
4. Turn in a 1cm (⅜in) seam allowance to the wrong side along the opening at the top.
5. Slip piece C, wrong side out, into the bag.
6. Pin the bottom fold to the seam joining pieces A and B, ensuring the corners line up, and pin the side seams. Check the height: it should reach the 2.5cm (1in) seam allowance of pieces A and B. Pin and tack/baste.

FINISHING

Attach the lining with invisible stitches catching each of the two fabrics alternately with the needle. Turn the bag the right way out and shape the corners.

Retors du Nord black 2005
—— 1 thread
━━ 2 threads

132 x 90 squares

1 square = 2 weft threads/2 warp threads

CAMELLIA BLOUSE

Revamp a white tunic with vintage charm and ignore all the rules of blackwork.

MATERIALS

* Linen tunic
* Natural cotton mix fabric: 30 x 30cm (11¾ x 11¾in)
* Retors du Nord black (2005) thread: 1 card
* Black button, 2.5cm (1in) in diameter
* Tracing paper and thick card
* Erasable textile pen
* Carbon paper for fabric
* Sewing and embroidery equipment

ONE SIZE

EMBROIDERY SIZE

Length of embroidery around neckline: approximately 1m (39½in)
Flower approximately 11cm (4¼in) in diameter (one petal: 5 x 5cm (2 x 2in))

STITCHES USED

Blouse:
stem stitch
chain stitch
wrapped running stitch

Flower:
stem stitch
chain stitch
fly stitch
straight stitch
wrapped running stitch

EMBROIDERY

The blouse

The design consists of a line embroidered around 4cm (1½in) from the seam of the neckline with motifs placed over and around it.

1. Trace motifs 1 and 2 (see pages 36 and 37). Make the templates from the card and cut out.
2. Draw the motifs onto the blouse with the marker pen; 4cm (1½in) from the seam of the neckline, draw a line that follows its curve.

> ### Tip
> *You can also use an iron-on motif pen to copy the motif.*

3. Use the templates to draw the outline of the motifs along the line, reversing their position and spacing them around 4.5cm (1¾in) apart. At the end of the line, finish off by drawing a teardrop shape. Embroider using wrapped running stitch (see page 8).
4. Embroider the motif in chain stitch and stem stitch using one strand of thread (see diagram below). When you reach the end, work the tails of thread into the underside.

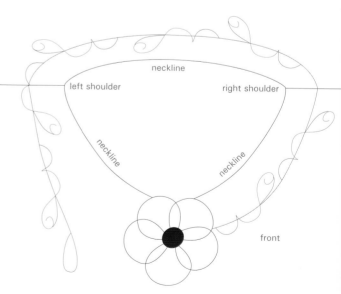

Petal A
Stem stitch

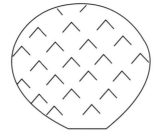

Petal B
Single fly stitch

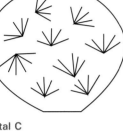

Petal C
Straight stitch

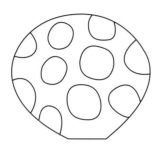

Petal D
Wrapped running stitch

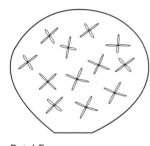

Petal E
Tight chain stitch

Retors du Nord. black 2005
—— 1 thread

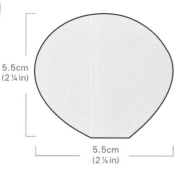

5.5cm
(2 ¼ in)

5.5cm
(2 ¼ in)

The flower

1. Trace one petal and cut out. Use this as a template for drawing 10 petals on the off-white fabric, spacing them 4cm (1 ½in) apart. Five petals will be used for the lining.
2. On petals B, C and E, mark where the stitches will start. You could also embroider randomly over the area.
3. Trace petals A and D with their motifs and transfer them to the fabric. Embroider the petals using the different stitches shown.

Making up the flower

1. When you have finished the embroidery, cut out each petal 1cm (⅜in) outside the line and finish the edges. Place one petal on each embroidered petal, pin together and tack/baste to hold in place. Sew, following the line that is visible on the lining.
2. Clip the edges, open out the seams and turn the right way out. Iron on the wrong side.
3. Form a fold at the bottom of each petal to make them more three-dimensional. Pin and sew up the fold 1mm (1/32in) from the edge for 1.5cm (⅝in), and work in the tail of the thread on the underside.
4. Overlap the petals to make the flower. Pin together and sew the centre of the flower together on the sewing machine, using straight and backstitch in different directions to hold all the petals together. Position the flower in the middle of the neckline at the front, at the point where the wrapped running stitch starts. Tack/baste and then sew to secure. Sew a button in the centre to hide the base of the assembled petals.

Tip

You can make flower brooches using the same motif by sewing an attachment to the back.

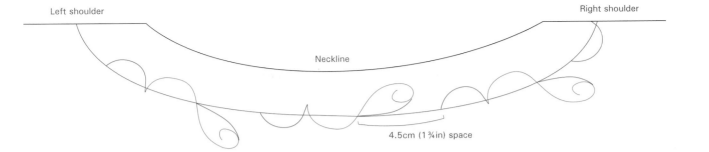

Left shoulder

Right shoulder

Neckline

4.5cm (1 ¾ in) space

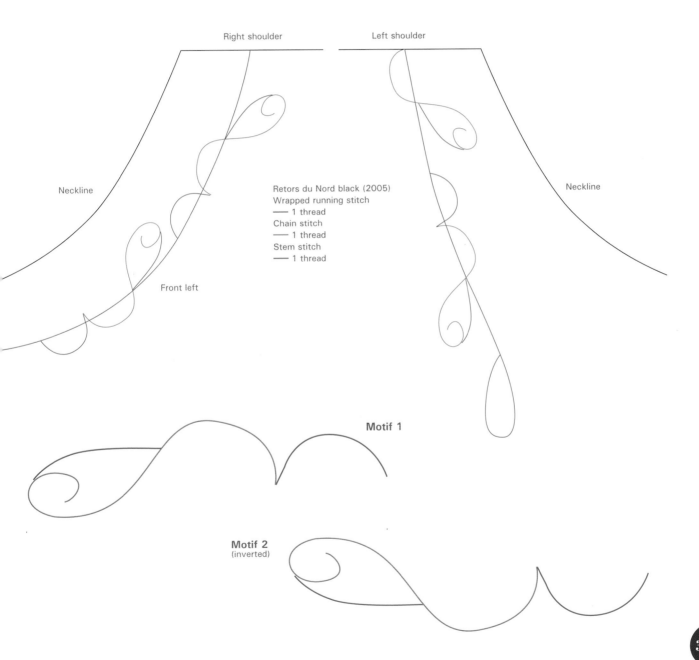

Right shoulder

Left shoulder

Neckline

Neckline

Retors du Nord black (2005)
Wrapped running stitch
— 1 thread
Chain stitch
— 1 thread
Stem stitch
— 1 thread

Front left

Motif 1

Motif 2
(inverted)

BLACK SAMPLER

Embroider twelve variations, find 48 buttons, make up, frame and admire.

⋯ MATERIALS ⋯

* Off-white linen fabric, 12 threads/cm (30 threads/in): 80 x 50cm (31½ x 19¾in)
* Natural cotton mix fabric: 40 x 54cm (15¾ x 21¼in)
* Retors du Nord black (6180) thread: 1 card
* 48 mother-of-pearl buttons, 0.5cm (¼in) in diameter
* Picture frame: 33 x 46cm (13 x 18in)
* Sewing and embroidery equipment

FINISHED SIZE

Each model: 6 x 7cm (2½ x 2¾in)
Frame: 32 x 46cm (12½ x 18in)

EMBROIDERY SIZE

Approximately 5.3 x 5.3cm (2 x 2in)

STITCHES USED

Holbein stitch

EMBROIDERY (diagrams on pages 40 and 41)

1. Cut twelve 16 x 16cm (6¼ x 6¼in) squares from the linen and finish the edges.
2. Mark the centre of the fabric with tacking/basting stitches and find the centre of the diagram by following the arrows on each side. Embroider in Holbein stitch.
3. Finish following the instructions on page 9.

MAKING UP

Prepare each square in the same way.

1. Working on the right side, mark the centre of the fabric, horizontally and vertically, with tacking/basting stitches.
2. Draw two cutting lines across the width, 2cm (¾in) above and below the embroidery. Cut the fabric along these lines and finish the edges (1). You now have a 16 x 9.3cm (6¼ x 3⅝in) rectangle.
3. To centre the embroidery in the final rectangle, measure from the tacked/basted lines in the middle and draw fold lines 3.2cm (1¼in) to either side and 3.5cm (1⅜in) above and below. Fold and press the folds with an iron. You now have a 6.5 x 7.3cm (2⅝ x 2⅞in) rectangle; finish the edges (2).

4. Fold in half widthways and sew up 1.5cm (⅝in) from the edge. Centre the seam on the wrong side in the middle of the back. Press the seams open with an iron and turn down a 1cm (⅜in) seam allowance along the top and bottom. Press with an iron, you now have a 6.5 x 7.3cm (2⅝ x 2⅞in) rectangle.
5. Turn the right way out, pin to secure the edges and use invisible stitches to close the openings at the top and bottom (2).

FINISHING

1. Finish the edges of the off-white fabric and tack/baste a line 4cm (1½in) from each side to define the working area.
2. Tack/baste a vertical line up the middle. Place four motifs on this line (3, page 40) – the first 4cm (1½in) from the bottom, the other three spaced 3cm (1¼in) apart.
3. Sew on one button at each corner. Refer to the diagram (page 40) for the placement of the other motifs. Frame your composition.

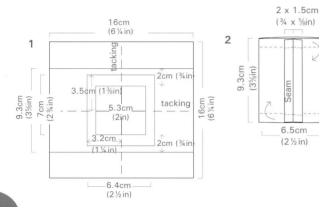

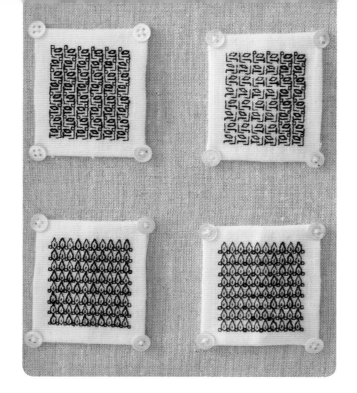

Positioning

3

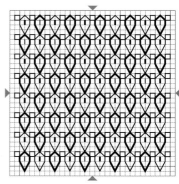

31 x 32 squares
6 x 6cm (2⅜in x 2⅜in)

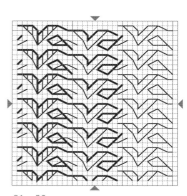

31 x 32 squares
6 x 6cm (2⅜in x 2⅜in)

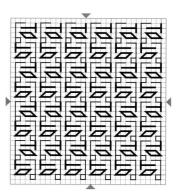

29 x 32 squares
4.8 x 5.1cm (1⅞in x 2in)

Positioning diagram labels:

4cm (1½in)   4cm (1½in)   4cm (1½in)

6.4cm (2½in)
7.3cm (2⅞in)

3cm (1¼in)   3cm (1¼in)   3cm (1¼in)

3cm (1¼in)   3cm (1¼in)   3cm (1¼in)

3cm (1¼in)   3cm (1¼in)   3cm (1¼in)

3cm (1¼in)   3cm (1¼in)   3cm (1¼in)

46cm (18¼in)

32cm (12⅝in)

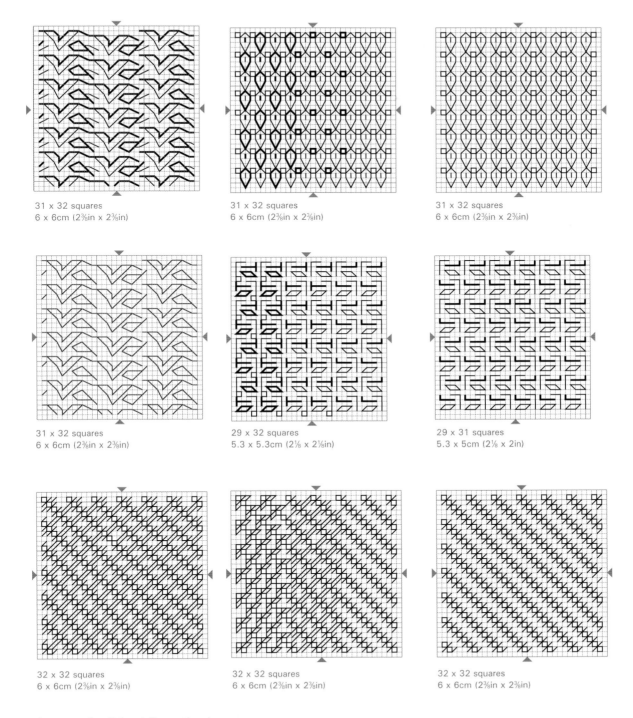

31 x 32 squares
6 x 6cm (2⅜in x 2⅜in)

31 x 32 squares
6 x 6cm (2⅜in x 2⅜in)

31 x 32 squares
6 x 6cm (2⅜in x 2⅜in)

31 x 32 squares
6 x 6cm (2⅜in x 2⅜in)

29 x 32 squares
5.3 x 5.3cm (2⅛ x 2⅛in)

29 x 31 squares
5.3 x 5cm (2⅛ x 2in)

32 x 32 squares
6 x 6cm (2⅜in x 2⅜in)

32 x 32 squares
6 x 6cm (2⅜in x 2⅜in)

32 x 32 squares
6 x 6cm (2⅜in x 2⅜in)

1 square = 2 weft threads/2 warp threads

Retors du Nord black 2005
—— 1 thread
—— 2 threads

A FISH ON MY SATCHEL

A whiff of holidays by the sea with this attractively customized satchel will make you dream of playing truant.

MATERIALS

* Raw linen fabric, 12 threads/cm (30 threads/in): 25 x 25cm (9¾ x 9¾in)
* Calais Cocoon black (6118) thread: 1 cocoon
* Wadding/batting: 20 x 20cm (7⅞ x 7⅞in)
* Fabric satchel
* Embroidery and sewing equipment

FINISHED SIZE

21 x 21cm (8¼ x 8¼in)

EMBROIDERY SIZE

16 x 16cm (6¼ x 6¼in)

STITCHES USED

Holbein stitch
Catch stitch

EMBROIDERY (diagram on page 45)

1. Mark the centre of the fabric with tacking/basting stitches, and find the centre of the diagram following the arrows on each side.
2. Embroider from the centre in Holbein stitch using one or two strands of thread.
3. Finish following the instructions on page 9.

MAKING UP

1. Working on the right side of piece A, draw cutting lines 3.5cm (1⅜in) from each side of the embroidery.
2. Cut the fabric along these lines to obtain a 23 x 23cm (9 x 9in) rectangle. Finish the edges.
3. On the wrong side of piece A, define the area to be padded by drawing a line 2cm (¾in) from each edge of the embroidery. Turn down the fabric along these lines following the grain of the fabric to obtain a 20 x 20cm (7⅞ x 7⅞in) rectangle.
4. Centre piece B (20 x 20cm (7⅞ x 7⅞in) wadding/batting) in the space marked out by the folds made previously, and tack/baste in place.
5. Turn in 1.5cm (⅝in) along the edges of the hem allowance following the grain of the fabric; mitre the corners (see page 9), iron on the wrong side to press in the folds and tack/baste to secure. You now have a 20 x 20cm (7⅞ x 7⅞in) square.
6. Catch stitch the hems to the wadding/batting, catching each of the two fabrics with the needle in turn.

FINISHING

1. Centre the embroidered square on the front of the satchel and pin and tack/baste to hold in place.
2. Use invisible stitches all round, catching the edge of the linen and the fabric of the satchel alternately.

1
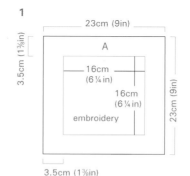

2
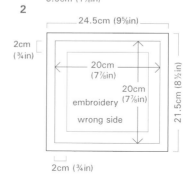
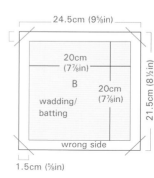

3

Mitred corner

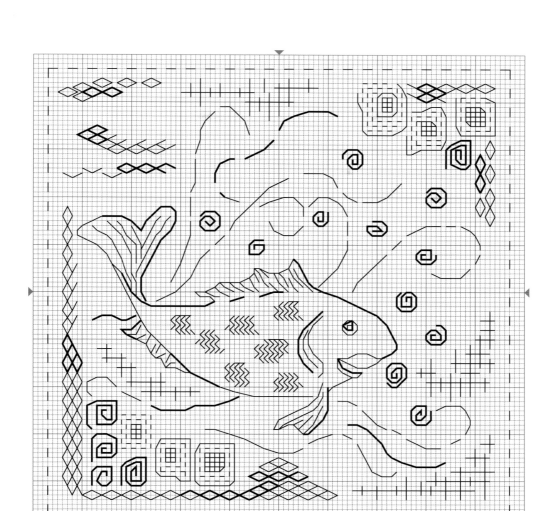

94 x 94 squares   1 square = 2 weft threads/2 warp threads

Holbein stitch
Calais Cocoon black (6180)
—— 1 thread
—— 2 threads

JOLLY TABLE MATS

Embroider coloured letters for a cheerful start to the day.

⁞ MATERIALS ⁞

* White linen fabric, 12 threads/cm (30 threads/in): 45 x 55cm (17¾ x 21¾in) (one mat)
* White cotton fabric: 26 x 21cm (10¼ x 8¼in)
* Retors du Nord: orange (2540), pink (2024), blue (2838), black (2005) thread: 1 card of each
* Sewing and embroidery equipment

FINISHED SIZE

42 x 32cm (16½ x 12½in)

EMBROIDERY SIZE

Mat 1: Chocolat: 20.3 x 4.5cm (8 x 1¾in), café: 10 x 4.5cm (4 x 1¾in), thé: 7.3 x 4.5cm (2⅞ x 1¾in)
Mat 2: Petit déjeuner: 35 x 6cm (13¾ x 2⅜in), léger: 12 x 6cm (4¾ x 2⅜in)

STITCHES USED

Holbein stitch
Backstitch

EMBROIDERY (diagrams on pages 48 and 49)

1. Finish the edges of the linen. Tack/baste lines 6.5cm (2⅝in) from the edges to mark the area to be embroidered (42 x 32cm (16½ x 12½in)).
2. Embroider each word in the positions shown on the diagrams. Count the threads of the fabric from the tacked/basted line, following the diagram to establish where each motif should start.
3. Start by embroidering the first or last letter, or the one in the centre depending on placement.
4. Finish following the instructions on page 9.

MAKING UP

1. Draw a line 3.5cm (1⅜in) inside the edges to mark the finished area of the mat. 6.5cm (2⅝in) remains around each side to form the hems.
2. Working round each side in turn, fold a 3.5cm (1⅜in) hem allowance to the right side along the tacking/basting line, and press with an iron. Open out the folds and working on the wrong side, prepare 3cm (1¼in) hems with a second 0.5cm (¼in) edge fold, and mitre the corners (see page 9).
3. Working on the wrong side of the mat, tack/baste all round the 0.5cm (¼in) folds, slip the lining under the hems and, centring it carefully, pin the edges in place to secure. Then stitch the hems invisibly to the lining and iron on the wrong side.

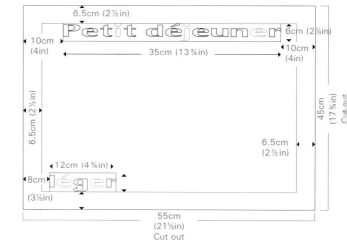

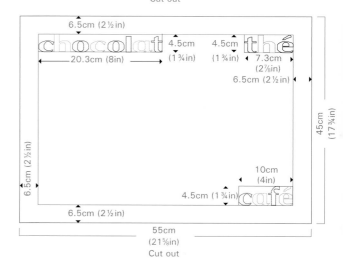

chocolat

thé

Petit déjeuner

café

léger

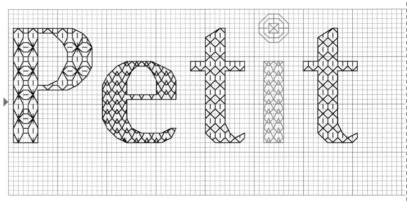

Motif to be embroidered at centre top
210 x 37 squares
35 x 6cm (13¾ x 2⅜in)

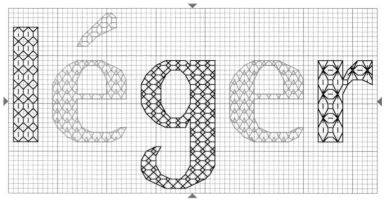

Tip

Before starting the embroidery, make sure you have tacked/basted lines around the area to be embroidered. This makes it much simpler to position the words correctly.

Motif to be embroidered at bottom left
73 x 37 squares
12 x 6cm (4¾ x 2⅜in)

1 square = 2 weft threads/2 warp threads

Outline of letters: backstitch
Inside pattern: Holbein stitch
— Black (2005): 1 thread
— Orange (2540): 1 thread
— Pink (2024): 1 thread
— Blue (2838): 1 thread

Motif to be embroidered at top left
213 x 27 squares
20.3 x 4.5cm (8 x 1¾in)

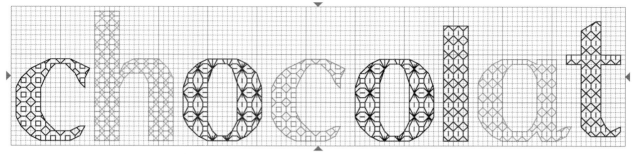

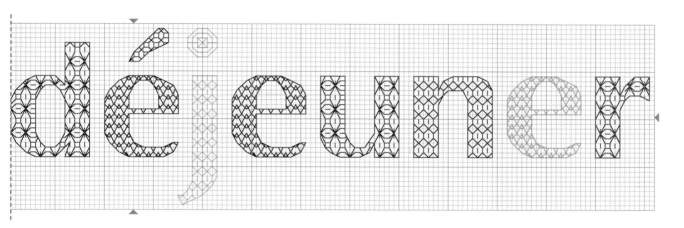

Motif to be embroidered at bottom right
61 x 27 squares
10 x 4.5cm (4 x 1 ¾ in)

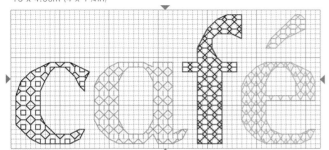

Motif to be embroidered at top right
46 x 27 squares
7.3 x 4.5cm (2⅞ x 1 ¾ in)

MOORISH BLANKET

A few stunning, contrasting squares on immaculate white and you are ready for your travels.

* White linen fabric, 12 threads/cm (30 threads/in): 120 x 140cm (47¼ x 55in)
* Calais Cocoon black (6180) thread: 2 cocoons
* Caudry Cocoon thread: black (3180) (3 cocoons), red (3434) (1 cocoon), garden (3051) (1 cocoon)
* Interfacing: 100 x 50cm (39⅜ x 19¾in)
* White blanket, 130 x 180cm (51¼ x 71in)
* Sewing and embroidery equipment

FINISHED SIZE

130 x 168cm (1½ x 1¾yds)

EMBROIDERY SIZE

Squares A 17.5 x 17.5cm (6⅞ x 6⅞in)
Squares B 20.5 x 20.5cm (8 x 8in)

STITCHES USED

Running stitch
Holbein stitch
Backstitch
Chain stitch
French knot
Catch stitch

EMBROIDERY (diagrams on pages 52 and 53)

1. Cut five 27 x 27cm (10¾ x 10¾in) squares and four 24 x 24cm (9½ x 9½in) squares from the linen and finish the edges.
2. Mark the centre of the fabric with tacking/basting stitches. Pinpoint the centre of the diagram by following the arrows on each side. Embroider five squares A, then four squares B using Holbein stitch.
3. Finish following the instructions on page 9.

MAKING UP

Square A

1. Working on the right side of piece A, draw cutting lines 2cm (¾in) from each side of the embroidery. Cut out the fabric along these lines to obtain a 21 x 21cm (8¼ x 8¼in) rectangle. Finish the edges (1).

2. On the wrong side of piece A, define the area to be interfaced by drawing a line four threads from the edge of the embroidered square. Fold the fabric along the grain on these lines, and press each fold to the wrong side with an iron (2).
3. Centre the interfacing, adhesive face down on the wrong side of the embroidery in the space marked by the folds made previously. Tack/baste into place and iron on. Fold back a 1.7cm (⅝in) seam allowance around each side, following the grain of the fabric, mitre the corners (see page 9), iron on the wrong side to press in the folds and tack/baste to secure. You now have a 17.5 x 17.5cm (6⅞ x 6⅞in) square (3).
4. Catch stitch the hems to the interfacing, catching the fabric and the interfacing with the needle in turn (4).

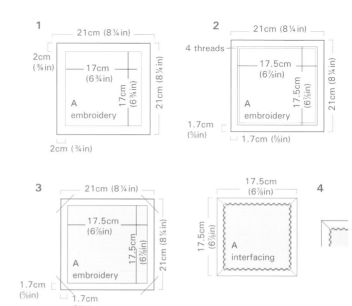

Square A
100 x 100 squares

1 square = 2 weft threads/
2 warp threads

Square B

1. Working on the right side of piece B, draw cutting lines 2cm (¾in) from each side of the embroidery. Cut the fabric along these lines to obtain a 24 x 24cm (9½ x 9½in) rectangle. Then finish the edges (1).

2. On the wrong side, define the area to be interfaced by drawing a line four threads from the edge of the embroidered square. Fold the fabric along the grain on these lines, and press each fold to the wrong side with an iron. Centre the 20.5 x 20.5cm (8 x 8in) interfacing, adhesive face down on the wrong side of the embroidery, then follow the instructions from point 3 of square A. You now have a 20.5 x 20.5cm (8 x 8in) square (2).

3. Form the hems in the same way as for square A (3).

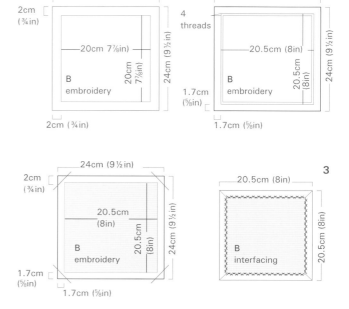

52

Square B
120 x 120 squares

1 square = 2 weft threads/2 warp threads

Calais cotton
Holbein stitch: —— Black 6180: 1 thread

Caudry cotton
Backstitch: —— Black 3180: 2 threads
Holbein stitch: —— Red 3434: 1 thread
                —— Lawn Green 3051: 1 thread
French knot: ● Black 3180: 1 thread
Chain stitch: ⬭ Black 3180: 1 thread
Work after finishing all the motifs, following the outline
of the empty space.

FINISHING

1. Place the squares randomly or symmetrically on the blanket.
2. Define the centre of the blanket by tacking/basting long stitches across the middle vertically, horizontally and diagonally using long stitches.
3. Centre one square A, then pin and tack/baste into place.
4. Arrange the other squares in accordance with square A, staggering them in relation to one another.
5. Use invisible stitches around each embroidery square, catching the edge of the fabric and the blanket in turn.

GIRL'S DRESS

An irresistible illustrated dress for a little girl.

···· MATERIALS ····························

* Raw linen fabric, 12 threads/cm (30 threads/in):
  92 x 50cm (36¼ x 19¾in)
* Calais Cocoon black (6118) thread: 1 cocoon
* Beige seam binding approximately 2m (79in)
* Paper for the pattern
* Erasable fabric pen
* Sewing and embroidery equipment

FINISHED SIZE

Size 2/3 years

Chest measurement 32cm (12½in) length
43cm (17in)

EMBROIDERY SIZE

25.5 x 5cm (10 x 2in)

STITCHES USED

Holbein stitch
Running stitch

EMBROIDERY (diagram on page 57)

1. Cut two 46 x 47cm (18 x 18½in) pieces from the linen. Finish the edges.
2. Mark the centre of each piece. Tack/baste straight up the middle; this will help to centre the embroidered motif around the bottom at the front as well as the pattern.
3. On one of the pieces, embroider the central motif, 7.5cm (3in) from the bottom, centring it across the width. Repeat the motif twice more, following the repeat on the pattern (see page 57). Embroider in Holbein stitch, starting from the central line of tacking/basting and from the midpoint of the diagram.
4. Work the ends of the threads in to the back of the embroidery by sliding the needle under the stitches.

Tip

When you have finished the embroidery, soak the work in water for 3 minutes to loosen up the fabric. Leave it to drip-dry; then while still damp, place on a towel and iron on the wrong side.

SEWING

Cutting (see pattern page 57)

The pattern provided is half the dress; the front and back are identical. The arrow on the pattern shows the fabric grain; it should run vertically up the height of the piece of fabric.
Trace the half pattern onto the two pieces of fabric, referring to the diagram on page 56 for the full length.

Front of dress

Work on the wrong side of the embroidery.
1. Fold the fabric in half lengthways along the central tacked/basted line and pin along the edge.

2. Place the top of the pattern 1.5cm (⅝in) from the upper edge – the middle line must be along the middle fold. Pin in place, taking in both layers of fabric. Draw the outline of the pattern in marker pen and draw a second line 1cm (⅜in) from the outline as your cutting line.
3. Cut out the piece along the line and finish the edges all round.
4. Follow the same process for the back.

MAKING UP

1. Lay the top on the back, right sides together; pin and tack/baste along the hem lines on the shoulders and sides to hold in place.
2. Sew the front and back together following the tacking/basting lines. Remove the tacking/basting.
3. Press open the seams on the wrong side with an iron.

FINISHING

Sewing

1. Tack/baste the seam binding around the neck opening, placing it on the right side of the fabric, around 3mm (⅛in) from the edge of the hem line. Cut an additional 1.5cm (⅝in) and turn in at the end.
2. Sew into place and fold the seam allowance to the wrong side, marking the fold in the fabric. Stitch the seam binding into place invisibly (see page 57).
3. Follow the same process for the armholes.

Embroidery

Highlight the hem line by embroidering along it in running stitch: insert the needle alternately over four threads and under two threads, sliding the needle through the thickness of the hem fold only so the running stitch is invisible on the wrong side.

You can also embroider the two little figures at the top and in the centre of the dress, or extend the pattern right around the dress.

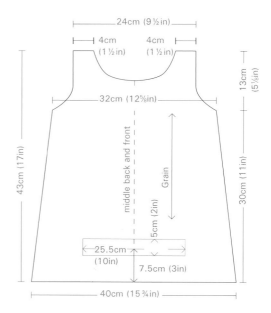

24cm (9½in)

4cm (1½in) 4cm (1½in)

32cm (12⅝in)

43cm (17in)

13cm (5⅛in)

middle back and front

Grain

30cm (11in)

25.5cm (10in)

5cm (2in)

7.5cm (3in)

40cm (15¾in)

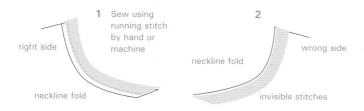

right side

1 Sew using running stitch by hand or machine

neckline fold

2

neckline fold

wrong side

invisible stitches

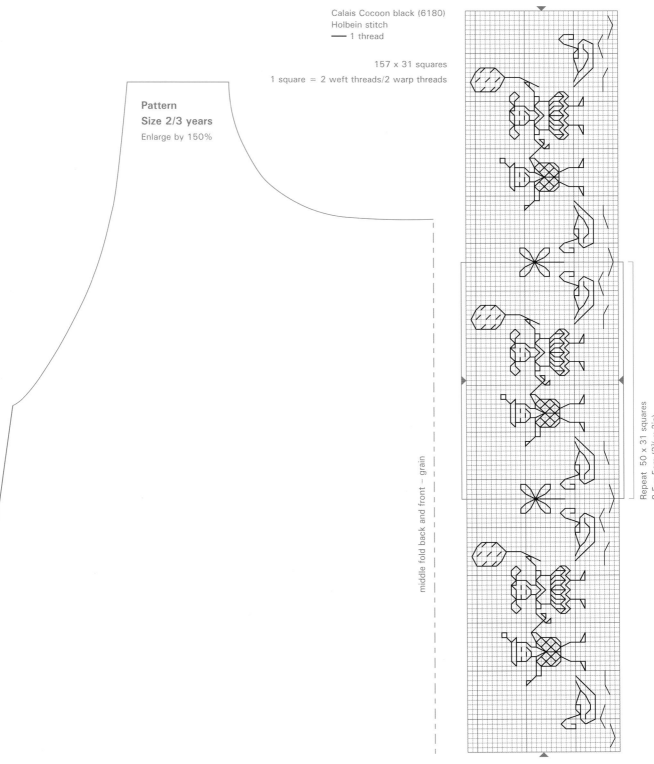

Calais Cocoon black (6180)
Holbein stitch
—— 1 thread

157 x 31 squares
1 square = 2 weft threads/2 warp threads

Pattern
Size 2/3 years
Enlarge by 150%

middle fold back and front – grain

Repeat 50 x 31 squares
8.5 x 5cm (3⅜ x 2in)

ELEGANT LITTLE MOUSE

This glamorous soft toy is sure to be a talking point.

···· **MATERIALS** ···············

* Cream linen fabric, 15 threads/cm (38 threads/in):
  65 x 55cm (25½ x 21¾in)
* Natural cotton mix fabric: 40 x 30cm (15¾ x 11¾in)
* Matching cotton lining: 28 x 11cm (11 x 4¼in)
* Wadding/batting: 10 x 12cm (4 x 4¾in)
* Retors du Nord black (2005) thread: 1 card
* Three matching beads
* Matching fancy button
* Two small black buttons
* 0.5cm (¼in) wide gingham ribbon: 20cm (7⅞in)
* Toy stuffing
* Embroidery and sewing equipment

FINISHED SIZE

25cm (10in) high

TEMPLATES PAGE 64

STITCHES USED

Running stitch
Daisy stitch
Fly stitch
Straight stitch
Chain stitch
Catch stitch

EMBROIDERY (diagrams on pages 60 and 61)

The skirt

1. Cut one 32 x 19cm (12½ x 7½in) rectangle from the linen and finish the edges. Mark the centre of the fabric vertically with tacking/basting stitches and pinpoint the centre of the diagram by following the arrows on each side.
2. Embroider the central motif of the border in running stitch, 2cm (¾in) from the edge. Highlight the motifs with chain stitch. Embroider the pattern 2.5cm (1in) above the border.

The blouse

1. Cut two 22 x 16cm (8¾ x 6¼in) rectangles (pieces A and B) to embroider for the front and back of the blouse and two 16 x 15cm (6¼ x 6in) rectangles (pieces C and D) for the sleeves. Finish the edges.
2. On piece A, embroider the front, marking the centre of the fabric with tacking/basting stitches. Embroider the border motif 2.5cm (1in) from the lower edge using running stitch and chain stitch, following the centre of the diagram. Embroider the lines in running stitch, then the motifs in running stitch, daisy stitch and straight stitch.
3. Embroider the back in the same way on piece B. Embroider the border motif 2.5cm (1in) from the lower edge, then six lines in total in straight stitch, leaving an equal space between each one.
4. Embroider the sleeves (pieces C and D), marking the centre of the fabric with tacking/basting stitches. Embroider the border motif 2.5cm (1in) from the bottom edge, then use running stitch to embroider the vertical lines.

MAKING UP THE SKIRT

1. Draw a vertical line 13cm (5in) high, 2cm (¾in) from the edge of the fabric, under the embroidered border. From the centre of the embroidery, draw a horizontal line 13cm (5⅛in) to either side. You now have a 26 x 13cm (10¼in x 5⅛in) rectangle. Cut along the lines and finish the edges.
2. Cut a 26 x 12cm (10¼in x 4¾in) rectangle from the lining material. Lay the two pieces right sides together and sew 1cm (⅜in) from the upper edge of the skirt; press the seams open with an iron. Fold the right sides together lengthways to sew the side seam. You now have a piece measuring 23 x 24cm (9 x 9½in). Sew 1cm (⅜in) from the edge, then press the seams open with an iron.
3. Hem the skirt on the wrong side: turn in a 1cm (⅜in) seam allowance under the embroidery, pin and catch stitch the hem into place. Fold the right side of the lining to the wrong side, adjust the length by folding a hem to the wrong side, iron and use invisible stitches on the hem of the skirt. Prepare the gathers around the top edge: sew a running stitch 5cm (2in) from the edge and repeat 0.3cm (⅛in) below. Do not tie off the threads.

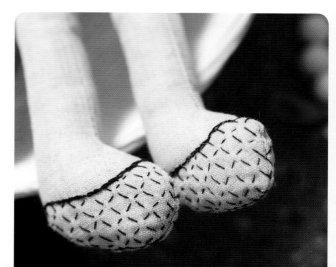

MAKING UP THE BLOUSE

The front and the back are identical.

1. Use the guide lines on the diagram (page opposite). Cut out the two pieces, centre them on the embroidery, draw around the edges and cut along the lines. Finish the edges and repeat for the back. Repeat for the sleeves.

2. Lay the two pieces right sides together, pin down the sides, lining up the embroidered base, and sew up the sides and across one shoulder 1cm (⅜in) from the edge. Leave an opening on the second: sew 0.5cm (¼in) from the armhole. Open the seams. Fold the sleeves down the middle, pin together lining up the embroidered base, and sew down the sides, 1cm (⅜in) from the edge.

3. Set in the sleeves: turn them the right way out, with the blouse the wrong way out. Mark a fold in the middle top of the armhole with a pin. Place the sleeve inside the blouse, line up the seams of the two parts, line up the mid-point marked by the pin on the shoulder seam and pin into place. Tack/baste around the armhole, then sew by hand 1cm (⅜in) from the edges using backstitch. Repeat to set in the other arm. Press open the seams with your nail and clip around the armholes.

4. Make up the hems (blouse and sleeves): mark a fold just under the embroidery, turn to the wrong side, sew up using invisible stitches and iron. Turn the right way out.

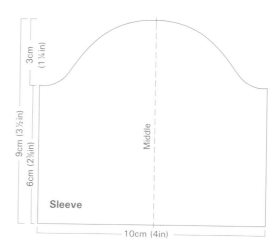

3cm (1¼in)

9cm (3½in)

6cm (2⅜in)

Middle

Sleeve

10cm (4in)

1cm (⅜in) seam allowances included

Sleeve

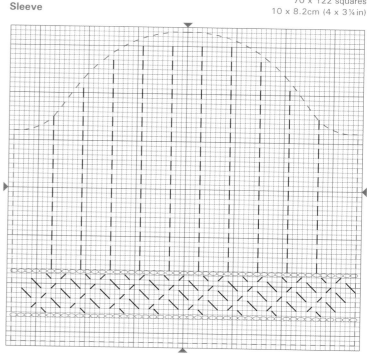

70 x 122 squares
10 x 8.2cm (4 x 3¼in)

Front and back

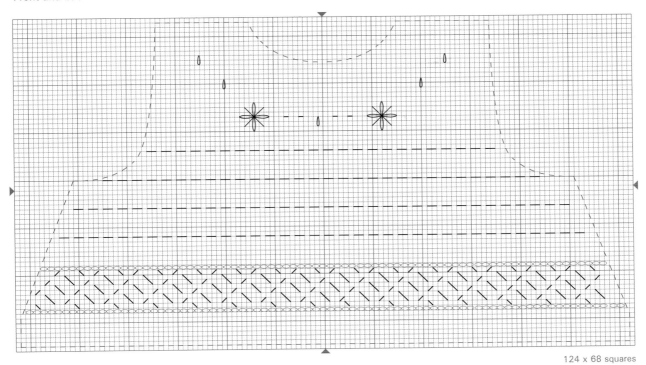

124 x 68 squares
8.2 x 4.5cm (3¼ x 1¾in)

Skirt

18 squares 2.5cm (1in)

18 squares
2.5cm (1in)

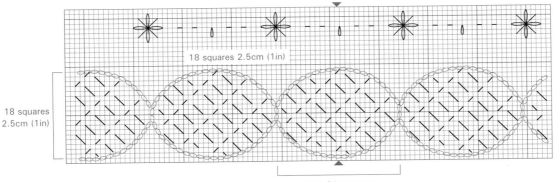

1 square = 2 weft threads/2 warp threads

repeat 24 squares

Retors du Nord black 2005
—— Running stitch: 1 thread
∞ Chain stitch: 1 thread
⬭ Daisy stitch: 1 thread

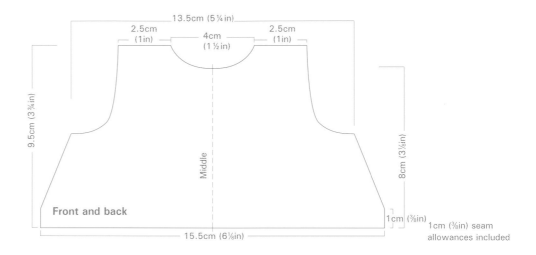

13.5cm (5¼in)

2.5cm (1in) 4cm (1½in) 2.5cm (1in)

9.5cm (3¾in)

Middle

8cm (3⅛in)

Front and back

1cm (⅜in)

1cm (⅜in) seam allowances included

15.5cm (6⅛in)

MAKING UP THE BODY

1. Draw two ears on the cotton mix fabric. Embroider using a tight chain stitch.

2. Cut two ears around the line on the wadding/batting. Line the wrong side of the embroidery with the wadding/batting and catch stitch into place.

3. Cut out the pattern pieces. Fold the cotton mix fabric in two and lay out the six pieces of the pattern, following the grain. Place the back of the legs and arms (twice) along the fabric fold as shown on the pattern. Draw round each piece and add the markers. Cut out 1cm (⅜in) outside the line and sew up along the line following the instructions below.

4. Make up the various parts in turn. Lay the two pieces of each arm and leg on top of each other, pin and sew along the line created by the extension of the fold, leaving the opening at the top. Pin the body together, sew along the seamline, leaving openings between the arm, leg and head markings.

5. Lay the two pieces for each ear (one of which is embroidered) right sides together, pin and sew along the line, leaving the opening. Repeat for the second ear.

6. Pin the back of the head and sew up the line without a marker. Pin the front of the head, sew up the front part of the line without markers. Pin the front and back of the head together and sew along the line, leaving openings between the ear and neck markers.

7. Attach the ears, working on the wrong side; clip the curves, turn the right way out and form the dart. Place them inside the head, embroidered side to the front, pin together round the opening and sew. Stuff the head.

8. Press open the seams with an iron, clip the curves and turn the various parts the right way out.

9. Stuff the arms, turn in a 1cm (⅜in) seam allowance along the opening and use invisible stitches to close. Position the under seams on the body, lining up the markers; then pin, tack/baste and sew on.

10. Stuff the legs, turn the seam to the front, turn in the seam allowance around the opening and use invisible stitches to close. Embroider the slippers using running stitch and highlight the top with chain stitch. Fasten off by working the threads into the thickness of the fabric. Centre the legs at the base of the body in line with the markers, spaced 1cm (⅜in) apart and pin, tack/baste and sew. Stuff the body, turn in a 0.5cm (¼in) seam allowance around the neck opening and tack/baste to hold in place.

11. Place the head at the top of the body, pin into place, tack/baste and sew on using invisible stitches, catching the material of the head and body with the needle in turn. Strengthen the seam by sewing back round it in the same way.

FINISHING

1. Dress the mouse; gather the top of the skirt by pulling on the threads that you left. Centre the seam at the back and sew the gathers to the body using invisible stitches.

2. Put on the mouse's blouse, sew up the shoulder seam with invisible stitches. Adjust the blouse, making a fold in the middle of the back; sew the fold in at the neck, and hold it in place down the back by sewing on three beads (see photograph on page 60).

3. Make a collar with the gingham ribbon: measure the neck hole, add a 0.5cm (¼in) seam allowance and cut two lengths A–B; place A under the neck hole, sew round using running stitch, place B on top, sew round using invisible stitches above and below.

4. Embroider the nose with satin stitch. Attach the eyes and the little button in the middle of the collar (see photograph, right).

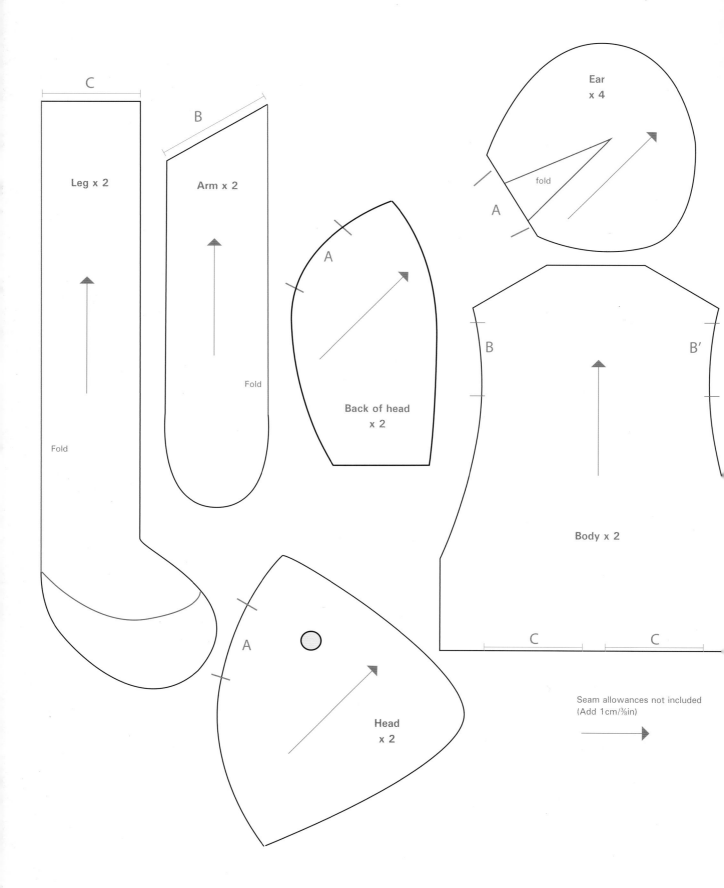

C

Leg x 2

Fold

Fold

B

Arm x 2

Fold

A

Back of head
x 2

Ear
x 4

fold

A

B

B'

fold

Body x 2

C

C

A

Head
x 2

A

Seam allowances not included
(Add 1cm/⅜in)